Receiving the Anointing
of the Spirit

VOLUME 6

Receiving *the* Anointing *of the* Spirit

Then after I have poured out my rains again, I will pour out my Spirit upon the people. Joel 2:28

....
A 30-day Devotional Bible Study for Individuals or Groups.
....

Dr. Larry Keefauver

CREATION
HOUSE
Orlando, FL

Receiving the Anointing of the Spirit by Larry Keefauver

Published by Creation House
Strang Communications Company
600 Rinehart Road
Lake Mary, FL 32746

Web site: http://www.creationhouse.com

Unless otherwise noted, all Scripture quotations are the Holy Bible, New Living
Translation, copyright © 1996. Used by permission of Tyndale House Publishers, Inc.,
Wheaton, IL 60189. All rights reserved.

78901234 87654321

Contents

Introduction

Welcome to this devotional study on *Receiving the Anointing of the Spirit* that will assist you in welcoming the Holy Spirit into your life. This is one of eight devotional studies related to the *Holy Spirit Encounter Bible*. Though not absolutely necessary, it is recommended that you obtain a copy of the *Holy Spirit Encounter Bible* for your personal use with this study guide. We make this recommendation because the same translation used in this guide, the *New Living Translation,* is also used in the *Holy Spirit Encounter Bible.*

It is also recommended that you choose the study guides in this series in the sequence that best meets your spiritual needs. So please don't feel that you must go through them in any particular order. Each study guide has been developed for individual, group, or class use.

Additional instruction has been included at the end of this guide for those desiring to use it in class or group settings.

Because the purpose of this guide is to help readers encounter the person of the Holy Spirit through the Scriptures, individuals going through it are invited to use it for personal daily devotional reading and study. Each daily devotional is structured to:

❖ Probe deeply into the Scriptures.

❖ Examine one's own personal relationship with the Holy Spirit.

❖ Discover biblical truths about the Holy Spirit.

❖ Encounter the Person of the Holy Spirit continually in one's daily walk with God.

We pray that this study guide will be an effective tool for equipping you to study God's Word and to encounter the wonderful third Person of the Triune God—the Holy Spirit.

*B*ut you are not like that, for the Holy Spirit has come upon you [you have an anointing from the Holy One], and all of you know the truth (1 John 2:20).

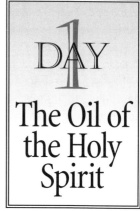

DAY 1
The Oil of the Holy Spirit

Anointing and oil are both symbols of the Holy Spirit consistently in Scripture. To *anoint* means, "to rub with," or "pour oil" upon someone or something. The name, Christ, or, Messiah, literally refers to, the Anointed One, God's Son, who is anointed by the Holy Spirit as God's chosen vessel to save and sanctify us.

In this study you will discover how the anointing in the Old Testament represented the person and ministry of the Holy Spirit who was poured upon all flesh on the day of Pentecost (Acts 2; Joel 2). The Old Covenant describes how oil was used in the practice of anointing to consecrate God's people for ministry and His vessels for worship. And the Old foreshadows the New (Heb. 10:1) through the fulfillment of the prophetic promises concerning the anointing of the Spirit who would come upon the Messiah to break mankind's yoke of sin and death (Isa. 53, 61). Through God's Anointed One, those who trusted in Jesus would be baptized and filled with the anointing oil of His Spirit.

Anointing oil was specially prepared in the Old Testament (Exod. 30:22–33) to be used in consecrating people and vessels for ministry. Read Exodus 30:22–33 and write down all the objects and people that were to be anointed:

_____

_____

John writes that those who have the spirit of antichrist oppose the body of Christ. So they are literally anti-anointing, anti-Holy Spirit, because they oppose all that the Anointed One represents. But those who trust Jesus are "little anointed ones," or "Christians," as we were first called in Acts 11:26, because the anointing of God flows within us.

How are you experiencing the anointing of the Holy Spirit right now in your life? Complete the following sentences:

When I encounter the anointing of the Spirit, I_____

_____.

The anointing means to me that _____

_____.

As a "little anointed one" I operate in the power of His anointing when _____

_____.

> *The anointing is not the exclusive possession of a few persons in leadership, it is the sanctifying flow of God's Spirit that empowers and sets His children apart.*

The anointing flows through all the Spirit does and produces to consecrate people and places that are holy unto the Lord.

Ask Yourself . . .

❖ In what ways has Jesus poured out His Spirit upon you for anointed service?

❖ Do you desire to be anointed and used fully by the Holy Spirit?

> *Write a prayer asking Jesus to pour out His Spirit upon you as an anointed vessel for His exclusive use:*

_____

_____

_____

_____

_____

*A*nd say to the people of Israel, "This will always be my holy anointing oil. It must never be poured on the body of an ordinary person, and you must never make any of it for yourselves. It is holy, and you must treat it as holy. Anyone who blends scented oil like it or puts any of it on someone who is not a priest will be cut off from the community" (Exod. 30:31–33).

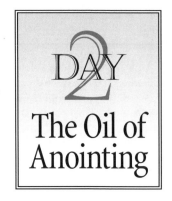

DAY 2
The Oil of Anointing

The anointing oil of the Old Covenant was specially prepared to set apart (make holy) God's priests, the tabernacle, and the vessels used in the tabernacle. It spoke of the Holy Spirit who has been specially prepared for those consecrated to the Lord's service.

God's priests under the New Covenant are His chosen called-out believers. We are His saints. And the oil of His Spirit is poured out and through the lives of Christians who have been set apart by Christ. Those born of the Spirit (John 3:3–8) are indwelt by the Holy Spirit (1 Cor. 6:19) and are consecrated human vessels named saints—His people *set apart* and *made holy* by the Spirit of God.

When you trusted in Jesus as your Lord and Savior, you were born again and given the gift of the Holy Spirit (Acts 2:38). At that moment, your designation as "sinner" was replaced with the anointing that made you a "saint." Read the passages below, then jot down what they say about the saints: [Note that in the *New Living Translation,* saints are also called *believers, holy people, Christians, and God's people.*]

Romand 8:27 _____

Romans 15:25 _____

1 Corinthians 1:2, 6:1–2, 14:33, 16:1 _____

2 Corinthians 9:12 _____

Ephesians 1:15–18, 2:19, 3:8, 4:12, 6:18 _____

Colossians 1:12, 26_____

2 Thessalonians 1:10 _____

Hebrews 6:10 _____

Revelation 5:8, 14:12, 15:3, 16:6, 19:8 _____

The same anointing that was on Christ from God's Spirit who resurrected Him, dwells in us as His saints (Rom. 8:11).

> *As a saint, you are anointed to do the works*
> *of Christ by the power of the Holy Spirit.*

Jesus declares, "The truth is, anyone [the saints] who believes in me will do the same works I have done, and even greater works, because I am going to be with the Father" (John 14:12). Put your name in the following blanks:

Saint _____ , you have been called and anointed by the Holy Spirit to be a holy and consecrated vessel in the hands of God. So as a Christian, "I _____ am a saint of the Most High God, and am anointed to be His ambassador on the earth.

Ask Yourself . . .

❖ How do you feel about being a saint, an anointed one in Christ Jesus?

❖ What reveals the anointing to those around you from your saintly life?

> *Write a prayer surrendering yourself to Christ's anointing and calling on your life as a saint:*

_____

_____

_____

_____

_____

*P*resent Aaron and his sons at the entrance of the Tabernacle, and wash them with water. Then put Aaron's tunic on him, along with the embroidered robe of the ephod, the ephod itself, the chestpiece, and the sash. And place on his head the turban with the gold medallion. Then take the anointing oil and pour it over his head (Exod. 29:4–7).

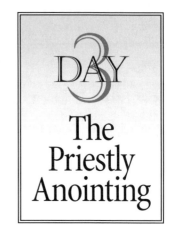

DAY 3

The Priestly Anointing

The anointing of Aaron the High Priest and his sons as Old Covenant priests foreshadowed the coming Anointed One who is our High Priest—Jesus Christ. Read Hebrews 8, then jot down all the ways Jesus ministers as our perfect High Priest:

_____

_____

_____

Jesus is described as the Anointed One and our eternal priest in Psalm 110. Now read this psalm, then list five ways Jesus rules as the Messiah, God's Anointed One:

1. _____

2. _____

3. _____

4. _____

5. _____

Notice that the High Priest in Exodus 29 was anointed by the pouring out of oil on his head. The oil then dripped down over his ears, eyes, noise, mouth, and face, then flowed down over his beard to his garments, and over the rest of his body.

This reminds us of how the Holy Spirit washes, cleanses, and baptizes us. Our bodies become living sacrifices as our minds are being renewed (Rom. 12:1–2). The mind of the priest is anointed before the rest of his body is sanctified and consecrated for service.

The Old Covenant priests' anointing symbolized a number of important truths that would be fullfilled in God's New Covenant priests (1 Peter 2:9–10). First, our minds are anointed so our thoughts are taken captive and renewed. When the anointing pours over our ears, we no longer listen to the voice of the world. Our ears hunger to hear God's voice. Next, when the anointing touches our eyes, we guard what we watch and read knowing that our eyes must be fixed on Jesus. Our mouths are also sanctified so what they speak and feed upon is the bread of life. And finally, our entire face is to reflect the glory of His anointing (2 Cor. 3:18).

Examine yourself. Is the oil of His anointing controlling your senses? Or, do you allow your senses to be filled with the corrupting acids of this world? Put an *x* on the line that represents where you are right now:

What I think about is
_____
Pure   Impure

What I hear is
_____
God's words   Worldly words

What I speak and feed upon is
_____
Bread of life   Stale bread

My gaze is fixed
_____
On Jesus   On the world

> *Like the Old Covenant priests, the anointing oil of God's Spirit must be poured upon you from head to toe so you are totally set apart for His service.*

The priestly anointing will lead you into a holy lifestyle of sacrifice, worship, and ministry. Such an anointing requires our total surrender and obedience to God's Spirit.

Don't regard lightly the priestly anointing. Anyone who seeks to minister independent from it imperils both himself and others. God's will on the issue is clear: "Be holy because I [the Lord] am holy" (Lev. 11:45).

Ask Yourself . . .

❖ Are you willing to minister as a holy priest under the anointing in Jesus' name?

❖ What worldly input into your life must you now reject as an anointed priest?

Write a prayer asking Jesus Christ's Spirit to anoint and empower you as His priest:

_____

_____

*S*o as David stood there among his brothers, Samuel took the olive oil he had brought and poured it on David's head. And the Spirit of the Lord came mightily upon him from that day on. Then Samuel returned to Ramah (1 Sam. 16:13).

DAY 4
The Kingly Anointing

First Peter 2:9 says, "You are a chosen people. You are a kingdom of priests, God's holy nation." Notice that God's word calls the saints of God a kingdom of priests or more literally: *a royal priesthood.* Jesus Christ is both High priest and King. So in Christ (Eph. 1:4), we are anointed as both priests and royalty. Jesus is King of kings and Lord of lords. And we are His family of royals over whom He rules.

Are you exercising your royal dominion by taking spiritual authority over the worldly spirits around you? Or are you letting yourself be oppressed by those made subject to you through the blood of Christ? Never forget that your position in Christ is royalty. In the Old Covenant, kings were anointed with oil to signify the power and presence of the Holy Spirit as well as His authority on their lives. So have you, under the New.

Are you living as a subject of this world or as royalty in Christ? Your position in Christ's anointing as royalty is described in the following passages. Read them, then jot down on the crown pictured below your kingly authority and position in Christ: [Eph. 1, Deut. 28, Col. 1, Rom. 5, 12; Josh. 1]

The kingly anointing on your life in Christ means that you are no longer a victim—you are a victor.

As a royal priest and king in Christ, you no longer have to be subject to and react to your circumstances—you can take control of your surroundings and possess the land in Jesus' name. Satan is under your heel (Rom. 16:20).

Below are some attributes of royalty. Circle the ones that you are walking in through the anointing, and underline those you have yet to understand and experience.

Authority	Power over the enemy
Royal Inheritance	Attitude of victory
Fortress and palace of safety	Powerful prayer
Feasting at the king's table	Bold access to God's throne
A family of princes and princesses	

Under the Spirit's kingly anointing, you have infinite resources and power to rule and reign in heavenly places.

Ask Yourself . . .

❖ Are you living daily as a prince or a pauper?

❖ Where do you need to start exercising your royal authority in life?

Write a prayer thanking Jesus for His royal anointing upon your life:

_____

_____

_____

_____

_____

A *nd the Lord came down in the cloud and spoke to Moses. He took some of the Spirit that was upon Moses and put it upon the seventy leaders. They prophesied as the Spirit rested upon them, but that was the only time it happened. (Num. 11:25)*

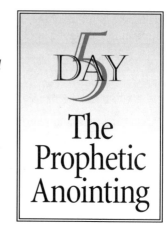

DAY 5

The Prophetic Anointing

The Spirit was poured out upon Moses and Elisha in a mighty way. Deuteronomy 34:10 says there was not a prophet in all of Israel like Moses with whom God spoke to face to face. Elijah had such a powerful presence of God's Spirit on his life that when it was time for his mantle of prophecy to be passed on to Elisha, God took Elijah up into heaven in a fiery chariot (2 Kings 2). But before Elijah left, Elisha asked him for a double portion of his spirit. Why? Elisha eagerly desired the prophetic anointing that God put upon Elijah to rest on him with a double portion of power and grace for ministry.

When Moses' anointing rested on the seventy elders of Israel, they prophesied. So there is an anointing that comes on the ministry of the prophet. But the prophetic anointing is most perfectly manifested in Jesus, the Anointed One, Christ.

> *In Jesus, we see the fullness of God's anointing to be Prophet, King, and Priest.*

A prophet speaks forth the Word of God. Jesus exemplified this anointing when He prophesied: "When you have lifted up the Son of Man on the cross, then you will realize that I am he and that I do nothing on my own, but I speak what the Father taught me" (John 8:28).

When the Holy Spirit has ministered to you through one who has a prophetic anointing, how have you received what the Father has said? Circle all that apply:

With thankfulness	In awe	Humbly
Joyfully	Fearfully	Skeptically
With doubt	Cautiiously	Other:_____

Paul describes how the prophetic anointing is to operate in the church in 1 Corinthians 14. Read this chapter, then mark the following statements true *T* or false *F*.

_____ Prophecy strengthens the church.

_____ Prophecy is greater and more useful than tongues when speaking to the whole church.

_____ In church it is better to speak ten thousand words in tongues than five prophetic words.

_____ Prophecy is for the benefit of believers only.

_____ Those who prophesy are in control and can wait their turn to speak.

_____ Prophecy should be given properly and in order.

(T, T, F, F, T, T)

The prophetic anointing carries with it tremendous responsibility and accountability. Because one who speaks the Word of the Lord must not only hear clearly what the Spirit is saying, he must also be responsible to always give all glory to Jesus Christ (1 John 4). All true prophecy comes from God, conforms to the Word of God, never attempts to take personal glory from the anointing, and always edifies the church.

Ask Yourself . . .

❖ How have you encountered the prophetic anointing?

❖ Is the Spirit desiring to speak a word from the Lord through you? When? To whom?

Write a prayer thanking the Holy Spirit for anointing prophets through the ages to speak clearly and boldly God's Word:

_____

_____

_____

_____

_____

*B*ut you are not like that, for you are a chosen people. You are a kingdom of priests, God's holy nation, his very own possession. This is so you can show others the goodness of God, for he called you out of the darkness into his wonderful light. "Once you were not a people; now you are the people of God. Once you received none of God's mercy; now you have received his mercy" (1 Peter 2:9–10).

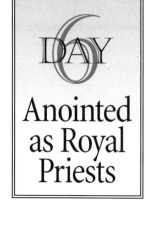

DAY 6

Anointed as Royal Priests

One of Satan's most persistent lies is that Christians are nobodies. He attacks us with such questions as:

- ❖ Who do you think you are anyway?
- ❖ Why would God use a person like you with your past?
- ❖ You aren't intelligent or strong—so why would God use you?

Satan has no new tactics. He relies on old lies and deceptions. But when we come to know the truth, the truth sets us free (John 8:32). Has Satan tried to make you feel like a nobody? Check any that apply:

❑ Brings up your past sins and failures.

❑ Brings strife and jealousy into your relationships.

❑ Tempts you to be hateful or bitter.

❑ Surrounds you with negative people.

❑ Steals your finances.

❑ Attacks you physically with illness.

❑ Tries to drain you emotionally.

❑ Tears down your self-esteem.

The Holy Spirit's anointing on your life makes you somebody. You are a priest and prince because you belong to God. This world and its things are under your feet. Below are some passages that confirm your victory in Christ Jesus. Read each passage, then jot down the promise of victory you have been given to destroy and overcome any attack of the enemy:

Romans 8:35–39 _____

Revelation 12:10–12 _____

John 16:16–33 _____

1 John 3:8 _____

Luke 10:16–22 _____

Psalm 37 _____

Psalm 91 _____

> *As royal priests, we are anointed with two mighty weapons of warfare—the Word and prayer.*

Jesus defeated Satan in the wilderness with the Word and prayer. The early church turned the world upside and boldly proclaimed the Gospel with the Word and prayer. So our priestly anointing is an armor of protection that prepares us to pray with power.

Read Ephesians 6:10–19 then complete the following sentences:

I use the sword of the Spirit, which is the Word of God when I _____

_____.

I use the weapon of prayer when I _____

_____.

To strengthen the Word in my life, I ask the Spirit to _____

_____.

To deepen prayer in my life, I ask the Spirit to _____

_____.

Since we have been anointed by the Spirit as a royal priesthood, we have the power to take back from the enemy anything he has stolen and to defeat his attacks at every turn. Paul declares this victory, "For I can do everything with the help of Christ [the Anointed One] who gives me the strength I need" (Phil. 4:13).

Ask Yourself . . .

❖ Are you tempted to believe Satan's lie that you are a nobody?

❖ Will you begin to claim through word and deed that you are anointed as a royal priest in Christ?

Write a prayer in your own words paraphrasing Philippians 4:13:

_____

_____

*T*hey were anointed and set apart to minister as priests (Num. 3:3).

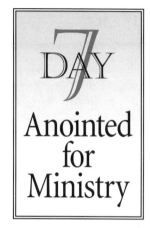

DAY 7
Anointed for Ministry

Ministry has a vertical and horizontal dimension. The Holy Spirit anoints us to minister first, vertically, unto the Lord. Jesus declared, "You must worship the Lord your God; serve only him" (Matt. 4:10; Deut. 6:13). We minister to the Lord when we worship and serve Him.

Once we minister vertically to the Lord we are anointed by His presence to minister horizontally to others. We minister the gifts of the Holy Spirit (1 Cor. 12, 14; Rom. 12; Eph. 4; 1 Peter 4). The Spirit's anointing for ministry makes us thirsty for His living water and overflows from out of us with His compassion for those in need.

> *As members of the body of Christ, we are a priesthood of believers anointed to minister to God and to one another.*

Describe how you encounter the Holy Spirit's anointing when He empowers you to minister vertically to God:

_____

_____

Describe the different ways the Spirit has empowered you to minister horizontally to others:

_____

_____

How do we know when ministry isn't anointed? There are many overt symptoms that warn us when a person is ministering out of their sinful nature instead of the Spirit's anointing. Here are some of those symptoms. Check any that you have observed personally in the church:

    ❏ Pride and seeking personal glory.

    ❏ Ignoring the real needs of the sheep to simply use and manipulate them for personal gain.

    ❏ Legalism and emphasis on religious traditions.

    ❏ Controlling people instead of releasing them into ministry.

❑ Emphasis on money and buildings instead of worship and service.

❑ Other: _____

The anointing for ministry in God's royal priesthood of believers fills His people with compassion and love for one another and the lost. Paul describes the ministry anointing in his letter to Timothy and Titus. Read the following passages, then jot down just a few qualities from each text that describes anointed ministry:

1 Timothy 3:1–13 _____

_____

1 Timothy 4:6–16 _____

_____

1 Timothy 6:2b–21 _____

_____

2 Timothy 2:1–26 _____

_____

2 Timothy 3:10–4:5 _____

_____

Titus 2 _____

_____

> *The anointing for ministry fills us with an unceasing desire to be in the presence of Jesus, to encounter His Holy Spirit, to minister His presence to others.*

Ask Yourself . . .

❖ Are your motivations for ministry pure and fixed on Jesus?

❖ In what ways are you anointed to minister?

> *Write a prayer thanking the Lord for all those who have ministered in anointed ways to you:*

_____

_____

*T*he leaders also presented dedication gifts
for the altar at the time it was anointed.
They each placed their gifts before the
altar (Num. 7:10).

Every vessel used in the Old Covenant tabernacle was anointed with oil and dedicated to
the Lord's use, including, and especially, the
altar of sacrifice. Everything we give and
sacrifice unto the Lord must come under the
anointing of the Holy Spirit to be wholly
accepted.

Anointing
for Sacrifice

> *Sacrificing just to sacrifice and giving
> just to give never serves God's purposes.*

God responded to the empty unanointed sacrifices and gifts of Israel during
Amos' day by pronouncing judgment. Read Amos 5:21–24, then summarize
what God says about sacrifices, offerings, and worship that are not anointed by
the Spirit:

_____

_____

God desires everything we offer Him to be anointed for sacrifice. So read the
following passages, then write down the kind of sacrificial anointing He desires
from us:

Psalm 51:16–17 _____

Acts 2:43–47 _____

Acts 4:32–37 _____

Romans 12:1–2 _____

2 Corinthians 9:6–15 _____

Galatians 2:20–21 _____

Are there any areas or things in your life that need to be placed on His anointed altar as a total accepted sacrifice? Write down those things, and through the
anointing of His Spirit surrender them totally to Christ:

_____

_____

The anointing for sacrifice is manifested in our lives when the Holy Spirit inspires us to surrender everything to Him. Partial surrender and sacrifice are never enough, so taking up our cross and following Jesus requires a genuine anointing on the sacrifice of our lives. True sacrificial living doesn't require the giving away of everything we have to live a monastic life. But it does require our surrender of everything the Lord gives us, understanding that we possess nothing, and that we are simply His stewards.

Jesus, the Anointed One, lived a sacrificial life. The anointed altar in the New Testament is the cross. As we accept His sacrifice and His Spirit's sacrificial anointing He fills us with the desire and a powerful commitment to follow Jesus wherever He leads. Read the following verses, and then jot down what is required of Jesus' disciples. And when you do, rejoice in the knowledge that the Spirit's anointing will empower you to do and to will everything you read:

Matthew 10:38 _____

Matthew 16:24 _____

Mark 8:31 _____

Mark 10:21 _____

Luke 14:27 _____

Galatians 6:14 _____

Ask Yourself . . .

❖ Are you willing to put everything you have and are on the Spirit's anointed altar of sacrifice?

❖ How has encountering the Holy Spirit changed your attitude toward sacrificial giving?

Write a prayer asking the Holy Spirit to anoint your life with the desire to live sacrificially for Christ:

_____

_____

_____

_____

A *nd no doubt you know that God anointed Jesus of Nazareth with the Holy Spirit and with power. Then Jesus went around doing good and healing all who were oppressed by the Devil, for God was with him (Acts 10:38).*

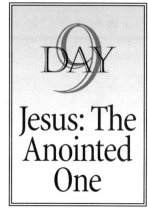

Jesus: The Anointed One

Christ, or Messiah, literally means *Anointed One.* The Holy Spirit conceived Jesus then poured Himself out on Jesus' life to empower Him for ministry. Jesus was born of the Spirit, then baptized and anointed in the Spirit to do mighty signs and wonders.

The Anointed One's anointing rests upon every believer to work in our lives the same way the anointing worked in His. Remember: "The Spirit of God, who raised Jesus from the dead, lives in you. And just as he raised Christ from the dead, he will give life to your mortal body by this same Spirit living within you" (Rom. 8:11).

Below is a review of how the anointing worked in God's Anointed One, and how His anointing works in His "little anointed ones"—Christians, like you. Look up the scriptures then match them with the right event.

Texts: Matthew 1:20; John 3:5; Matthew 3:16–17; Acts 2:38–39; Luke 4:18–19; 1 Corinthians 12:4–7; Romans 1:4; Romans 8:11.

The Spirit's Anointing on Jesus . . .	**The Spirit's Anointing on Us**
Jesus was born of the Spirit.	We are born of the Spirit.
text: _____	text: _____
Jesus was anointed at baptism.	We are anointed at baptism.
text: _____	text: _____
Jesus was anointed to minister.	We are anointed to minister.
text: _____	text: _____
Jesus was raised by the Spirit.	We are raised by the Spirit.
text: _____	text: _____

Jesus the Anointed One imparts His anointing in us. In the coming days, you will discover that each aspect of your relationship—*with, in, through, like, and to*—Christ is filled with His anointing. Because in Christ is the fullness of the Spirit's anointing, and when we are in Him, His anointing abides in us.

> *When others look upon our lives, they are to see Jesus' anointing and presence in us.*

To the right is a mirror. Read 2 Corinthians 3:16–18 then write on it all the qualities of Christ that your life reflects. [For a reference point, also read Galatians 5:22–23.]

When we live in the anointing, the Spirit of God empowers us to live like Jesus in the world. Others will see Him in us because the anointing always reflects Jesus.

Ask Yourself . . .

❖ Is everything you say and do a reflection of the Anointed One—Jesus Christ?

❖ How does Jesus' anointing empower you to minister as He did to others?

Write a prayer asking Jesus to pour out His anointing upon all of your actions, thoughts, attitudes, and feelings so others will see Him in everything you do:

_____

_____

_____

_____

_____

*I*t is God who gives us, along with you, the ability to stand firm for [in] Christ. He has commissioned us, and he has identified us as his own by placing the Holy Spirit in our hearts as the first installment of everything he will give us (2 Cor. 1:21–22).

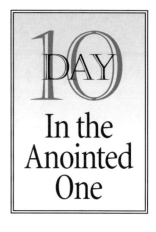

In the Anointed One

To be *in Christ* is to be in His anointing, power, and presence. Outside of Christ there is no life, no salvation, and no healing. But in Him, all things are held together (Col. 1:15–17).

In the anointing of the Anointed One we discover many blessings and benefits. Draw a line from the verses below to their matching benefits:

In Christ's anointing we have . . .	Texts
Love	2 Corinthians 5:19
One Body	Romans 8:39
Wisdom	2 Timothy 2:10
Faith	Romans 12:5
Reconciliation	Colossians 1:4
Glory	1 Timothy 3:13
Favor	Galatians 2:4
Peace	Philippians 4:7
Riches	Ephesians 3:8
Life	1 Corinthians 1:30
Treasures	2 Timothy 2:1
Confidence	Galatians 2:16
Unity	John 10:10
Freedom	Philippians 4:19

The anointing of Christ in His Spirit indwells us when we partake of His living bread. "All who eat my flesh and drink my blood remain in me, and I in them" (John 6:56).

The power of Christ's anointing who dwells in us is revealed in Luke 4:18–19 and Isaiah 61:1–3. Complete these sentences:

I have encountered His anointing to proclaim good news when _____

_____.

I have encountered His anointing to comfort the brokenhearted when _____

_____.

I have encountered His anointing to set captives free when _____

_____.

> *Christ rubs and pours out Himself upon us through*
> *His Spirit so we exude His grace and power in Him.*

No matter how old it is, an olive tree has leaves that always shine with oil because of the overflow within it. In a parallel way, the longer we live in Jesus, the more His spiritual anointing oil overflows, refreshes, and renews our lives.

Consider the treasure of the Spirit you have through your anointing *in Christ.* You have abundant life in Christ (John 10:10). And because the overflow of Christ's anointing is unlimited and continual, staying in Him assures the constant outpouring of His Spirit.

Ask Yourself . . .

❖ What area of your life in Christ is overflowing with His anointing?

❖ How is Christ using you as a vessel of ministry?

> *Write a prayer thanking Christ for all the benefits of being anointed in*
> *Him:*

_____

_____

_____

_____

_____

*F*or you died when Christ died, and your real life is hidden with Christ in God (Col. 3:3).

DAY 11

With the Anointed One

Christ hides our life with Him when He pours out His anointing upon us. *With Him* indicates that we encounter in Christ's anointing everything that He encountered in His life, death, and resurrection. We participate with Him in baptism, burial, and our new life through the power of the Holy Spirit.

Read the following verses, then write down after each of them how we actually live with the Anointed One:

Romans 6:3 _____

Romans 6:4 _____

Romans 6:6–8 _____

Romans 7:4 _____

Galatians 3:27 _____

Colossians 2:10–13 _____

Colossians 2:20 _____

Colossians 3:1–3 _____

We also participate *with Christ* in His sufferings.

> *The anointing brings us an acute awareness of the pain and suffering Jesus experienced.*

Read Philippians 3:10–11, then rewrite it by paraphrasing it in your own words:

_____

_____

The anointing of God's Spirit empowers us to encounter and experience Christ's suffering on the cross for the sins of the world. Because the anointing fills us with compassion for those who suffer, we can identify with the sufferings of others in the anointing and are compelled to help relieve them with the good news of Christ.

Suffering with Christ has given you compassion for. . . Check all that apply:

- ❏ The homeless
- ❏ The sick
- ❏ The lonely
- ❏ The lost
- ❏ The addicted
- ❏ The orphaned
- ❏ The abused

- ❏ The poor
- ❏ The imprisoned
- ❏ The brokenhearted
- ❏ Those in spiritual bondage
- ❏ The elderly
- ❏ The unborn
- ❏ The emotionally hurting

With Christ, we seek a hurting world from His perspective. People are needful, lost, and dying. We are moved by the Spirit to apply His leading and forgiveness to every need we encounter.

Ask Yourself . . .

❖ How does suffering *with Christ* change you and allow His anointing to flow through you to others?

❖ How are you experiencing life *with* the Anointed One?

Write a prayer asking Christ to anoint you with the fellowship of His suffering:

_____

_____

_____

_____

_____

*F*or all of God's promises have been fulfilled in him. That is why we say "Amen" when we give glory to God through Christ (2 Cor. 1:20).

The anointing *through Christ* points us to everything He has accomplished on our behalf. Through Christ's anointing, we have been saved, healed, and delivered. *Through the Anointed One* we have forgiveness of sin and eternal life. *Through Him* we give glory to the Father.

DAY 12
Through the Anointed One

> We can't worship or praise God the Father
> except through the anointing of Christ Jesus.

Below is a list of everything that has resulted in our lives through the Anointed One. Read each of the following scriptures, then check each listed blessing as you thank your heavenly Father for each of them bestowed through the Son.

_____ Authority and privilege (Rom. 1:5)

_____ Eternal life (Rom. 6:23)

_____ Freedom from sin (Rom. 8:2)

_____ Overwhelming victory (Rom. 8:37)

_____ Comfort (2 Cor. 1:6, 7)

_____ Confidence (2 Cor. 3:4)

_____ Righteousness (2 Cor. 5:21)

_____ Favor and kindness (Eph. 2:7)

_____ Forgiveness (Eph. 4:31–32)

_____ The prize (Phil. 3:14)

_____ Love and kindness (2 Tim. 1:9)

We encounter supernatural results in our lives through Christ's anointing for inner change, confidence, and new life.

We also have boldness through Christ to come before God's throne (Heb. 10). And the anointing *through Christ* is so powerful that we can do all things *through Him*.

Read Philippians 4:10–14, 19, and begin to claim the fulfillment of those promises that come *through Christ.* Say aloud the following declarations:

> ❖ *Through Christ I can be content in all circumstances.*
> ❖ *Though Christ I can do all things.*
> ❖ *Through Christ all my needs are met.*

Now examine your life carefully in light of these declarations. Circle the one hardest for you to claim and underline the one you need the most in your life right now.

The bondages that keep His promises from being fulfilled in our lives are broken *through the Anointed One, Christ.* Later we will discover how the anointing breaks the yoke of every bondage in our lives (Isa. 10:27; Luke 4:18). But for now, identify where in your life you need a breakthrough of Christ's anointing. Check all that apply:

I need the breakthrough of His anointing in my:

❑ Finances

❑ Family

❑ Marriage

❑ Church

❑ Work

❑ Relationships

❑ Ministry

❑ Other: _____

Ask Yourself . . .

❖ What hinders the breakthrough of Christ's anointing in your life?

❖ Will you allow every promise of God to you to be fulfilled through the Anointed One?

> *Write a praying asking the Holy Spirit to break every bondage in your life through Christ:*

_____

_____

A *nd all of us have had that veil removed so that we can be mirrors that brightly reflect the glory of the Lord. And as the Spirit of the Lord works within us, we become more and more like him and reflect his glory even more (2 Cor. 3:18).*

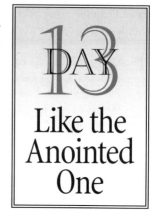

DAY 13
Like the Anointed One

The Holy Spirit is constantly desiring to conform us to the image of Jesus Christ. We were created in God's image, but the Fall shattered that image and we lost the glory that once crowned us. But the Anointed One who was conceived by the Holy Spirit restored all of humanity's potential to once again be crowned in that glory that was always intended by God (Ps. 8:5; John 1:14).

We are *becomers* because we haven't yet reached perfection or maturity. So we are sojourners being changed into God's likeness in our life journey as we grow away from our sinful natures toward the perfection of the Spirit in Christ (Rom. 8).

> We are becoming like the Anointed One.

Chart your course on this journey. Put an *x* on each line below to indicate how far along you are in this transformation of becoming more and more *like Christ.*

Sinner   Saint

Broken   Whole

Lost   Restored

Profane   Holy

Impure   Pure

The transformation that we encounter in the Spirit's anointing involves both change and risk. But at times, even though we know the outcome is our transformation in Christ, we resist change because we fear the unknown.

How are you responding to the change and transformation happening in you as a result of the anointing? Complete these sentences:

What I fear the most as the Spirit transforms me is _____

_____.

The change He desires in me that I resist most is _____

_____.

I am excited about being transformed in _____

_____.

The transformation from glory to glory into Christ's likeness continues throughout our lives. And when He returns in glory, we shall be completely like Him. Read 1 John 3:2 and rewrite it in your own words:

_____

_____

Ask Yourself . . .

❖ What is the most significant area of change in your life right now being produced by the work of His anointing?

❖ Are you fully yielded to the anointing's transforming power?

Write a prayer praising God for transforming you by His Spirit from glory to glory into the likeness of Christ:

_____

_____

_____

_____

_____

*I*f anyone gives you even a cup of water because you belong to the Messiah, I assure you, that person will be rewarded (Mark 9:41).

The anointing settles the eternal question: "To whom or what do I belong?" That to which we belong establishes our identity. *Belonging to* a certain family gives us our name and biological background. *Belonging to* a certain church makes us a Baptist, Methodist, Pentecostal, Charismatic, etc. *Belonging to* a certain country club makes us middle class, upper class, or whatever.

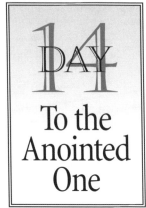

DAY 14

To the Anointed One

Belonging to anything in the natural connects us with others to form relationships, but only gives us a superficial identity that can be changed or lost in a moment's notice. *Belonging to the Messiah,* however, seals our identity forever. "And now you also have heard the truth, the Good News that God saves you. And when you believed in Christ [the Anointed One], he identified you as his own by giving you the Holy Spirit, whom he promised long ago" (Eph. 1:13).

> *The Holy Spirit seals your identity as one who belongs to the Anointed One.*

We live, move, and have our being in the anointing of Jesus.

Read the following passages, then write down the identity each one says you have in the Anointed One, Christ:

My identity forever is . . .	Text
_____	John 1:12
_____	John 15:15; Romans 5:10
_____	Galatians 4:28
_____	Philippians 2:5–11
_____	1 Peter 2:9

Belonging meets one of our deepest needs—to be accepted and loved. So Christ joined Himself to us to share His position and power with us as God's adopted sons.

Read the following Scripture, and underline each word or phrase that reveals a benefit or blessing we receive because of belonging to the Anointed One:

In the Anointed One, We are . . .

But God is so rich in mercy, and he loved us so very much,
that even while we were dead because of our sins,
he gave us life when he raised Christ from the dead.
(It is only by God's special favor that you have been saved!)
For he raised us from the dead along with Christ,
and we are seated with him in the heavenly realms—
all because we are one with Christ Jesus.
And so God can always point to us as examples
of the incredible wealth of his favor and kindness
toward us, as shown in all he has done for us
through Christ Jesus.
God saved you by his special favor when you believed.
And you can't take credit for this;
it is a gift from God.
Salvation is not a reward for the good things we have done,
so none of us can boast about it.
For we are God's masterpiece.
He has created us anew in Christ Jesus,
so that we can do the good things he planned for us long ago.
—Ephesians 2:4–10

Ask Yourself . . .

❖ What feelings do you have about the assurance of belonging to the Anointed One?

❖ How does belonging to Christ eliminate insecurities in your life?

Write a prayer praising Christ for the joy of belonging to Him:

_____

_____

*T*he priest will also pour some of the olive oil into the palm of his own left hand. He will dip his right finger into the oil and sprinkle some of it seven times before the Lord. The priest will then put some of the olive oil from his hand on the lobe of the person's right ear, on the thumb of the right hand, and on the big toe of the right foot, in addition to the blood of the guilt offering. The oil that is still in the priest's hand will then be poured over the person's head. In this way, the priest will make atonement for the person being cleansed (Lev. 14:26–29).

The Oil of Cleansing

This remarkable description of just one step of the leper's healing anointing in the Old Testament typifies how we as sinners are cleansed from sin, just as lepers were consecrated and cleansed under the Old Covenant. When a leper presented himself to a priest for cleansing, he had to remove all clothing, shave all the hair from his body, and bathe in water. Then the priest would examine the former leper, pronounce him clean, and anoint him with blood and oil.

Applying this to our lives in Christ, we are stripped of our old life to put on the new (2 Cor. 5:17). We are washed in baptism through dying to self and are raised in Christ as our spirits are renewed (Rom. 6:1–11). We are cleansed by the blood of Christ (1 John 1:7) and are anointed by His Spirit (Acts 2:38).

To make this typology clearer, let's explore the application of the three places a cleansed leper was anointed. First, the ear was anointed. The ear represents whatever we listen to and allow into our minds. That's why Jesus often said, "Anyone who is willing to hear should listen to the Spirit and understand what the Spirit is saying to the churches" (Rev. 3:13; John 4:24).

The anointing of the Spirit counsels us in what we should listen to and what we should guard against in our walk with Christ. Write down those things that the anointing helps us to guard against hearing (i.e., profanity, pornography, etc.):

The anointing helps us guard against hearing . . .

1. _____

2. _____

3. _____

4. _____

5. _____

Next, the priest anointed the right thumb of the cleansed person. That represents our work and service. Jesus declared, "Let your good deeds shine out for all to see, so that everyone will praise your heavenly Father" (Matt. 5:16). On the hands to the left, write down some of the good deeds the Holy Spirit is empowering you to do:

Then, the priest anointed the right toe. This represents our walk in the Spirit. On the foot to the right above, write the direction and purpose the Spirit is leading you in:

Finally, the priest poured the anointing oil over the head of the cleansed person indicating that the cleansing was completed and the person was free of all disease.

> *In Christ's anointing, we have been set free from the leprosy of sin to live consecrated to Him.*

Ask Yourself . . .

❖ Which area of your life most needs His anointing?

❖ How are you living out your cleansing and freedom in Christ?

Write a prayer thanking Jesus for pouring the oil of His Spirit over all of your life:

_____

_____

_____

*Y*ou are the light of the world—like a city on a mountain, glowing in the night for all to see. Don't hide your light under a basket! Instead, put it on a stand and let it shine for all. In the same way, let your good deeds shine out for all to see, so that everyone will praise your heavenly Father (Matt. 5:14–16).

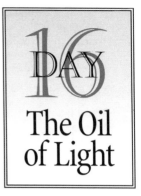

DAY 16
The Oil of Light

The oil in the Old Covenant tabernacle lampstand represented the fiery presence of the Holy Spirit. But today under the New Covenant, Christ's believers are God's temple and lampstands. We are God's lights that shine Jesus' brightness everywhere in the world.

The oil in the tabernacle lampstand was to be tended continually so the light would never be extinguished. Likewise, the anointing of the Spirit in our lives ignites us continually as we shine for Christ. Jesus is the light of the world (John 8:12). So when He sends us the Holy Spirit—the oil of His presence—He continually ignites His oil in our hearts so we burn night and day for Him.

How have you burned brightly for Christ during the last week. Write down some of the ways you have allowed your light to be seen:

_____

_____

_____

The flame of the Spirit's oil burning brightly in us makes us children of light.

> *The anointing puts our lives in God's spotlight.*

The world takes notice of Christians. We're watched closely to see if our walk is consistent with our talk.

Ephesians 4:17–5:14 describes in detail what a true life on fire with the anointing is like. Read these scriptures, then put a check next to the qualities listed below that are possessed by Christ's children of light. Check all that describe your life:

❑ Sexual purity

❑ No obscene stories, foolish talk, or coarse jokes

❑ Thankfulness to God

- ❏ Not greedy
- ❏ Righteous, holy, and truthful
- ❏ Anger doesn't control
- ❏ Do honest work
- ❏ Don't use foul or profane language
- ❏ Encourage others
- ❏ Rid self of bitterness
- ❏ Kind to others
- ❏ Forgiving of others
- ❏ Doesn't try to excuse sin

Now look over those qualities you haven't checked and ask the Holy Spirit to anoint you to begin shining in those areas of your life.

Ask Yourself . . .

❖ In what way has the fire of God's Spirit shined in your life today?

❖ How will you shine for Jesus in the lives of others who live presently in darkness?

Write a prayer seeking the fire of God's Spirit to anoint you in power as you share Christ in the world:

_____

_____

_____

_____

_____

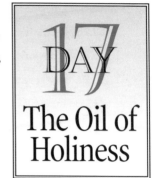

A *nd say to the people of Israel, "This will always be my holy anointing oil. It must never be poured on the body of an ordinary person, and you must never make any of it for yourselves. It is holy, and you must treat it as holy. Anyone who blends scented oil like it or puts any of it on someone who is not a priest will be cut off from the community"* *(Exod. 30:31–33).*

Day 17
The Oil of Holiness

The anointing oil used in the Old Covenant was regarded as holy—set apart unto the Lord. It was pure, consecrated. And since the oil was holy, anything or anyone anointed with it was made holy. Nothing about this anointing oil was commonplace or ordinary. It was specially made and kept for ministry by the priests because it symbolized the Spirit who would anoint every believer under the New.

When the oil of the Holy Spirit anoints our lives, we are holy because He imparts His holiness to us. He makes us pure and sets us apart for God's exclusive use. Holiness is not a goal that we attain, it is an act of grace applied by the Holy Spirit through the shed blood of Jesus Christ.

> *The anointing requires that we live holy lives.*

Read the following passages, then write down what the New Testament reveals about the requirement of holiness for the saints—His holy ones.

John 17:17 _____

Romans 6:19–22 _____

1 Corinthians 1:2, 30 _____

1 Corinthians 3:17 _____

Ephesians 4:24 _____

Colossians 1:12, 3:12 _____

1 Thessalonians 4:3–7 _____

2 Timothy 1:9 _____

1 Peter 1:15 _____

Notice that the anointing oil in the Old Testament was specially prepared then kept from worldly contamination. In the same way, the outpouring of the Spirit's anointing today consecrates us and makes us holy.

But to continually walk holy, our lives must be disciplined by the Spirit so we keep ourselves from world contamination. We must continually guard our hearts and minds from temptation and pride.

List five tempting things you must deliberately avoid in order to live in holiness.

1. _____

2. _____

3. _____

4. _____

5. _____

We need the help of the Holy Spirit to resist sin in our lives, because we can't keep ourselves holy without His power and grace. His anointing on Scripture and in the lives of others can help to keep us pure.

Below is a list of ways the Holy Spirit works to keep us holy. Rank from 1 (most often) to 5 (least often) that which He uses to keep you holy and pure:

_____ Accountability to another Christian family member or friend

_____ Study and application of the Word of God

_____ Worshiping often with the body of Christ

_____ Fellowshiping with other believers

_____ Praying and seeking the face of God

_____ Other: _____

Ask Yourself . . .

❖ How are you yielding to the Holy Spirit to keep yourself pure and avoid temptation?

❖ In what ways does the Holy Spirit work in your life to produce holiness?

Write a prayer seeking the Spirit's anointing of holiness in your daily walk:

_____

_____

_____

*O*ne day the widow of one of Elisha's fellow prophets came to Elisha and cried out to him, "My husband who served you is dead, and you know how he feared the Lord. But now a creditor has come, threatening to take my two sons as slaves."

"What can I do to help you?" Elisha asked. "Tell me, what do you have in the house?"

"Nothing at all, except a flask of olive oil," she replied.

And Elisha said, "Borrow as many empty jars as you can from your friends and neighbors.

Then go into your house with your sons and shut the door behind you. Pour olive oil from your flask into the jars, setting the jars aside as they are filled."

So she did as she was told. Her sons brought many jars to her, and she filled one after another. Soon every container was full to the brim!

"Bring me another jar," she said to one of her sons.

"There aren't any more!" he told her. And then the olive oil stopped flowing. When she told the man of God what had happened, he said to her, "Now sell the olive oil and pay your debts, and there will be enough money left over to support you and your sons" (2 Kings 4:1–7).

Like the widow in this story, we may not realize that with God's Spirit, a little is much. The miraculous use of oil in it reminds us of the anointing. So let's discover some truths about the oil of God's Spirit from this widow's account. Consider the following insights, and complete the sentences that conclude each point.

1. *When we have nothing except the anointing, we have enough.*

The widow saw nothing in the house to meet any of her deepest needs except a flask of olive oil. But that was enough! So, like her, when we have nothing except the Holy Spirit's anointing, we have enough. When we are at the end of our resources, we are ready for a miracle. Because the anointing won't manifest our needs as long as we can.

How will the anointing meet your need? Read Zechariah 4:6. When my

strength is not enough, then _____.

2. *The anointing needs empty vessels.*

The widow was told by the man of God to find as many empty vessels as possible. And when she did, the overflow of the oil from the first vessel filled all the remaining empty vessels and didn't cease until there were no empty vessels left. In the same way, the anointing uses us when we're empty vessels. He

pours Himself out into every vessel that will empty itself of pride and self.
Read Psalm 51:8–17. For the Spirit to pour Himself into me, I must empty

myself of _____.

3. *The anointing fills every vessel completely.*

The widow discovered that she could fill every empty vessel to the brim.
Likewise, the anointing also fills every believer completely up. But the Spirit won't
share space within us with anything or anyone because God is a jealous God and
we are holy, consecrated, and dedicated vessels to be used totally by Him.
Read Ephesians 5:18. The Spirit is filling me so He may _____

_____

4. *The anointing meets every need.*

Finally, the widow's account shows us that when there are no empty vessels,
the anointing stops flowing. When members of the body of Christ become too
prideful and full of self to minister to one another's needs and the needs of the
world, the Spirit's anointing ceases to flow because the anointing flows through
us to meet the needs of others.
Read 1 Corinthians 12:1–11, 26. The anointing fills me so I am empowered to

_____

Ask Yourself . . .

❖ Are you emptying yourself continually and always seeking the overflow of
the Spirit's anointing?

❖ How is the anointing empowering you to minister to others today?

*Write a prayer asking Christ to overflow you with the anointing so you can
minister to others:*

_____

_____

_____

_____

*Y*ou prepare a feast for me in the presence of my enemies. You welcome me as a guest, anointing my head with oil. My cup overflows with blessings (Ps. 23:5).

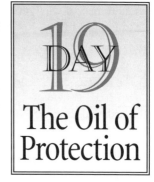

The Oil of Protection

In the ancient Middle East, one's home was understood to be a sanctuary for a guest. Hospitality dictated that sojourners were to be sheltered, fed, and protected as guests by the head of the house. So a guest would always be honored and esteemed. After he was washed and cleansed from the journey, the ancient eastern guest was anointed with oil and his every need was provided for. If he had any enemies lying in wait outside the door or the city gate, he was safe inside his host's house because the home was an honored sanctuary.

In a similar way, the anointing oil of the Spirit makes us a guest in the Father's house (John 14:2, 23). With His Spirit's presence comes His anointing. And with His anointing comes His protection and blessings. Because His anointing breaks every yoke of bondage and slavery in our lives (Isa. 10:27; Luke 4:18).

> *The Spirit's protective anointing guides and directs our paths as we obey His voice.*

The Holy Spirit speaks Jesus' words to His sheep so they will hear and be protected from the enemy. Jesus describes this anointing for His protection in John 10. Read the passage below and underline each phrase that reveals how our Good Shepherd protects His sheep:

> *I assure you, anyone who sneaks over the wall*
> *of a sheepfold, rather than going through the gate,*
> *must surely be a thief and a robber!*
> *For a shepherd enters through the gate.*
> *The gatekeeper opens the gate for him,*
> *and the sheep hear his voice and come to him.*
> *He calls his own sheep by name and leads them out.*
> *After he has gathered his own flock,*
> *he walks ahead of them, and they follow him*
> *because they recognize his voice.*
>
> *They won't follow a stranger;*
> *they will run from him because*
> *they don't recognize his voice.*

Those who heard Jesus use this illustration
didn't understand what he meant,
so he explained it to them. "I assure you,
I am the gate for the sheep," he said.
"All others who came before me were thieves and robbers.
But the true sheep did not listen to them.
Yes, I am the gate.

Those who come in through me will be saved.
Wherever they go, they will find green pastures.
The thief's purpose is to steal and kill and destroy.
My purpose is to give life in all its fullness.
I am the good shepherd.
The good shepherd lays down his life for the sheep.
A hired hand will run when he sees a wolf coming.
He will leave the sheep because they aren't his
and he isn't their shepherd.

And so the wolf attacks them and scatters the flock.
The hired hand runs away because he is merely hired
and has no real concern for the sheep.
I am the good shepherd; I know my own sheep,
and they know me, just as my Father knows me
and I know the Father. And I lay down my life for the sheep.
I have other sheep, too, that are not in this sheepfold.
I must bring them also, and they will listen to my voice;
and there will be one flock with one shepherd."
—John 10:1–16

Ask Yourself . . .

❖ Are you trying to protect yourself, or are you under the protection of His anointing?

❖ What kind of witness is your life to your enemies? Are they seeing you victorious under His protective anointing while you eat at His table of abundance?

Write a prayer thanking Christ for His protective anointing over your life because of your sanctuary in the Father's house:

_____

_____

*I*n that day the Lord will end the bondage of his people. He will break the yoke of slavery and lift it from their shoulders [Note: This additional phrase is included in the NKJV—And the yoke will be destroyed because of the anointing oil.] (Isa. 10:27).

DAY 20

The Oil of Power

The Lord protects his people and gives victory to his anointed king. (Ps. 28:8)

The anointing destroys any burden or bondage and gives us the Spirit's power to defeat any foe. Victory, liberty, and freedom are in the anointing. "It is not by force nor by strength, but by my Spirit, says the Lord Almighty" (Zech. 4:6).

On the lines below, write every burden or bondage the Spirit's anointing of power has broken and defeated in your life:

_____

_____

_____

The anointing not only has power to break bondages, it will also work miraculous signs and wonders that point to Jesus Christ as Lord and give honor and glory to God.

Take some time to reflect on any signs and wonders you've seen manifested under the anointing of God's Spirit. Below is a list of some different manifestations of the Spirit's signs and wonders. Write down a brief description of each that you have witnessed:

Physical healing _____

Deliverance _____

Emotional healing _____

Relationship healed _____

Financial miracle _____

Miracle in nature or creation _____

Other: _____

Signs and wonders result from the anointing of power the Holy Spirit pours out upon God's people.

The power to do God's work rests in the anointing of His Holy Spirit. That's why we can do nothing except by His anointing.

After the Spirit's anointing was poured out in power on the day of Pentecost (Acts 2), signs and wonders flowed freely through the church. Read the following scriptures that describe His acts on Pentecost, then write down the sign or wonder evidenced by the Anointed One's powerful gift.

Acts 2:4–12 _____

Acts 2:47 _____

Acts 3:1–10, 4:22 _____

Acts 4:31 _____

Acts 4:33 _____

Acts 5:12–16 _____

Acts 6:7 _____

Acts 6:10 _____

Acts 7:55–56 _____

Acts 8:14–25 _____

Acts 8:26–40 _____

Ask Yourself . . .

❖ What evidence of the Spirit's anointing and power have you been seeing in your life recently? In your church?

❖ Are you willing to allow the Holy Spirit to work powerfully through you with signs and wonders, even if it means persecution and hardship?

Write a prayer asking the Lord to anoint your life with His oil of power:

_____

_____

_____

_____

_____

Y*ou love what is right and hate what is wrong. Therefore God, your God, has anointed you, pouring out the oil of joy on you more than on anyone else (Heb. 1:9).*

God poured out His anointing of joy upon Jesus, His Anointed One. And since we, God's children, are *in* Christ, we partake of His outpouring of joy. So in this study we will spend some time in three different sections to gain a better understanding of how to keep this anointing of joy.

DAY 21

The Oil of Joy

1. *He (the Spirit) that is in you is greater than he that is in the world (1 John 4).*

Therefore, nothing in this world can overcome the anointing. But that doesn't mean it won't be challenged. What tries to steal your joy? Check all that apply:

❑ Financial problems   ❑ My enemies

❑ Work difficulties   ❑ Hypocrites at church

❑ The media reporting all the bad news   ❑ Negative people

❑ Others who dump their problems on me ❑ Other: _____

Regardless of what you checked, nothing on the list above has the power to defeat your anointing of joy.

2. *Because the anointing can overcome anything in this world, the only way you can lose your joy is to give it away.*

That's right! If your joy has been stolen, then you let it go. It was you who chose to be depressed. It was you who decided to lose or give up. Because Jesus declared, "No one can rob you of that joy" (John 16:22). So it is us who forfeit the anointing when tempted to give in.

When do you feel most tempted to give in and give up your anointing of joy? Rank from 1 (greatest temptation) to 5 (least temptation).

_____ When I am physically tired.

_____ When I am emotionally drained.

_____ When I feel alone.

_____ When I get a bad attitude.

_____ When I am not being fed spiritually.

_____ Other: _____

3. *Giving up on ourselves and even on others doesn't rob us of joy.*

The truth of the matter is we lose our joy when we give up on Christ. Why? He is the source of our anointing. He replaces all mourning with joy. Read Isaiah 61:1–3, then describe how the Anointed One gives us joy:

_____

_____

Jesus' life was filled with the joy of the Holy Spirit (Luke 10:21). And He fills our lives with the same joy. How? Jesus overcame the world through His cross and resurrection.

> *Jesus' victory released the anointing of joy into our lives so we can praise Him and rejoice even when circumstances appear grim.*

Because the victory has already been won through the cross and resurrection, not even death can rob us of our joy in Christ (1 Cor. 15:54–58).

Ask Yourself . . .

❖ Have you given away your joy instead of claiming your victory in Christ?

❖ How can you share Christ's joy with others who are contemplating giving up?

Write a prayer of joy in Christ:

_____

_____

_____

_____

_____

O *n the day Aaron and his sons are anointed, they must bring to the Lord an offering (Lev. 6:19).*

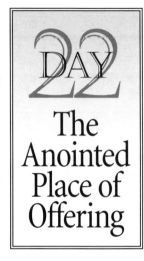

DAY 22
The Anointed Place of Offering

What a powerful principle this is for us in Leviticus. It teaches us that encountering the anointing requires our willingness to give the Lord an offering. It's not that we pay for the anointing, we simply respond with thanksgiving for what the Lord has done.

God is a giver. So when we encounter the anointing of His Spirit, we are prompted to be givers like Him. We respond to His anointing with an attitude of gratitude because we know His anointing is an act of grace, an act of giving on His part. And that we can do nothing to earn or deserve the anointing. So recognizing the anointing as a gift, we respond joyfully and thankfully by giving God the offering of our lives.

Read the following texts then list the offerings from our lives we can make joyfully and thankfully to God:

Romans 12:1–2 _____

Mark 12:33 _____

1 Corinthians 16:2 _____

2 Corinthians 5:21 _____

Philippians 2:17 _____

Hebrews 13:15 _____

1 Peter 2:5 _____

Some try to buy the anointing believing if they establish a place of offering that it will become a place of anointing. Read the story of Simon in Acts 8:9–25, then answer the following questions:

Why did the Spirit's anointing impress Simon? _____

_____

What did Simon want for himself? _____

_____

What did he offer for what he wanted? _____

_____

> *When we enter into the anointing, we are filled with the joy of giving.*

The anointing is poured out upon us so we may pour ourselves out as a drink offering for others. Having received so much from the Lord, we want to give so others may receive.

The only profit one receives from the anointing is souls added to the kingdom of God. The only recognition that comes with the anointing is the glory given to God.

The moment Aaron and his sons received the anointing, they entered into the anointed place of offering; so do we.

Has the anointing of the Holy Spirit been poured out upon your life? If you can answer "Yes," then complete these sentences:

Because I have been anointed, I can give _____

_____.

The anointed place of offering gives me joy in sharing _____

_____.

I receive the most joy when I offer God my _____

_____.

Ask Yourself . . .

❖ How can I offer my life more completely to God?

❖ How can I share the anointing with others?

> *Read Psalm 54:6, then write a prayer praising God for the opportunity to give Him your life as an offering:*

_____

_____

_____

*T*hen Jacob woke up and said, "Surely the Lord is in this place, and I wasn't even aware of it." He was afraid and said, "What an awesome place this is! It is none other than the house of God—the gateway to heaven!" The next morning he got up very early. He took the stone he had used as a pillow and set it upright as a memorial pillar. Then he poured olive oil over it. He named the place Bethel—"house of God"— though the name of the nearby village was Luz (Gen. 28:16–19).

Jacob anointed the place where he met with God in prayer and named it *Bethel*, "the house of God." Similarly, wherever we meet with God, that is our anointed place of prayer.

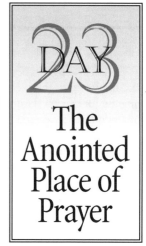

DAY 23

The Anointed Place of Prayer

Both prayer and the place we pray are anointed because of the presence of the Spirit of God. When God met with Moses at the burning bush with His fiery presence He consecrated it as "holy ground" (Exod. 3:5). The threshing floor that David bought from Araunah was an anointed place of prayer. David built an altar there (2 Sam. 24:18–25). And Solomon built his temple there (2 Chron. 3:1). The site was ancient Mount Moriah upon which Abraham had built his altar to sacrifice Isaac his son (Gen. 22). This place was certainly an anointed place of prayer!

There is nothing inherent in a place that makes it anointed. But when the oil of the Spirit is poured out in an area where God and man meet, the place becomes anointed.

Where is your holy ground? Where do you meet with God regularly?

List the places where you meet with God regularly in order of frequency.

1. _____

2. _____

3. _____

4. _____

5. _____

There is an anointed place of prayer that far outweighs any natural place in both significance and frequency of use. That anointed place of prayer is the heart. So wherever we pray is an anointed place.

Paul wrote, "I pray that from his glorious, unlimited resources he will give you mighty inner strength through His Holy Spirit. And I pray that Christ will be more and more at home in your hearts as you trust in him. May your roots go down deep into the soil of God's marvelous love" (Eph. 3:16–17).

Deep within your new heart given by His Spirit (Ezek. 36:26; Jer. 31:33–34) is the anointed place of prayer where the Spirit prays for us (Rom. 8:26–27). In the heart below, describe how the Spirit prays within and through you:

Ask Yourself . . .

❖ Are you meeting often enough at your anointed place of prayer?

❖ How is the Spirit praying in and through you?

Go to an anointed place of prayer and yield to the Holy Spirit there as He prays through you.

_____

_____

_____

_____

_____

*T*he Kingdom of Heaven can be illustrated by the story of ten bridesmaids who took their lamps and went to meet the bridegroom. Five of them were foolish, and five were wise. The five who were foolish took no oil for their lamps, but the other five were wise enough to take along extra oil . . . But while they [foolish]] were gone to buy oil, the bridegroom came, and those who were ready went in with him to the marriage feast, and the door was locked . . . So stay awake and be prepared, because you do not know the day or hour of my return (Matt. 25:1–13).

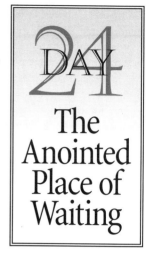

Day 24
The Anointed Place of Waiting

Jesus taught this parable to keep His people alert in the Spirit and ready for His return. Those not abiding and waiting in the Spirit will find themselves lacking when the Bridegroom comes. But those ready to meet Him will be waiting and filled with His Spirit. This is not only true concerning Christ's return for His bride in the future, but for each individual Christian who personally faces meeting Jesus at any moment in life.

Isaiah prophesied that those who wait upon the Lord will find new strength (Isa. 40:31). So the anointed place of waiting for Christ is never a place of listlessness or laziness. To wait doesn't mean to be idle. Rather, it denotes a perseverance in prayer, worship, and service under the anointing of His Spirit. The Hebrew word for *wait* in Isaiah 40:31 (*qavah*) means "to bind together, to look for hope, expect." So we persevere no matter how much time passes in our waiting as we look for the Lord.

How do feel when you're in the anointed place of waiting and persevering? Circle the feelings you have:

Peace	Joy	Relaxed
Tense	Anxious	Hopeful
Expectant	Tired	Stressed
Frustrated	Impatient	Other:_____

The anointed place of waiting both conditions and strengthens us. "But those who wait upon the Lord will find new strength. They will fly high on wings like eagles. They will run and not grow weary. They will walk and not faint" (Isa. 40:31).

And the anointed place of waiting is a place of inner peace no matter how violently the storms of life rage around us. Paul writes about such a place in

Philippians 4:4–20. Read this passage, then complete the following sentences:

I worry most when _____

_____.

The anointing helps me overcome worry when _____

_____.

Waiting and staying alert for me are _____

_____.

When my circumstances are most difficult, I usually _____

_____.

When I wait upon the Lord, my thoughts are _____

_____.

The place the Spirit anoints for our waiting is a place where faith is refined, love is deepened, and hope is built. Such a place becomes a citadel of confidence that is able to withstand every onslaught of unbelief.

Ask Yourself . . .

❖ Are you abiding in the place of His anointing? Are you alert and waiting for the Lord?

❖ How have you grown spiritually over the years from your encounters with the Spirit in your seasons of waiting?

Write a prayer asking Christ to keep you alert and ready for Him in the anointed place of waiting:

_____

_____

_____

_____

_____

*T*he Spirit of the Sovereign Lord is upon me,
because the Lord has appointed me to bring
good news to the poor. He has sent me to comfort
the brokenhearted and to announce that captives will be
released and prisoners will be freed. He has sent me to
tell those who mourn that the time of the Lord's favor
has come, and with it, the day of God's anger against
their enemies. To all who mourn in Israel, he will give
beauty for ashes, joy instead of mourning, praise instead
of despair. For the Lord has planted them like strong
and graceful oaks for his own glory (Isa. 61:1–3).

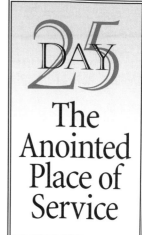

DAY 25
The Anointed Place of Service

The anointed place of service is called "ministry,"
and it doesn't involve natural position, title, or
power. Those who seek for power and position in
the human halls of ministry will discover that this
sort of humanly-earned endeavor has no anointing.

> *The anointed place of service is a place of outpouring—the*
> *outpouring of God's Spirit upon those who need ministry.*

So where is the anointed place of service? And who are those who need it?

1. *Those who are anointed serve the poor.*

They serve the poor in spirit (Matt. 5:3) because the poor in spirit lack God's
abundant life (John 10:10). So you will find the poor in the anointed place of
service.

The poor whom I serve through the power of the anointing are _____

_____.

2. *Those who are anointed serve the downtrodden (Luke 4:18).*

Those whose inner lives have been shattered by worldly battering rams of fear,
worry, deprivation, loneliness, and rejection are in desperate need of ministry.
The Holy Spirit uses us—wounded healers—to bind up and pour the oil of
healing over the wounds of the downtrodden. So the downtrodden will also be
found in the anointed place of service.

The downtrodden that I will go to and bind up their wounds are_____

_____.

3. *Those who are anointed set free the captives (Luke 4:18).*

There are many who need deliverance from demons that haunt and oppress. So the bondages of sin and guilt are broken by the anointing. And the captives who need their freedom will be found by those anointed to serve in the Anointed One's place.

Those captives I will set free In Jesus' name are _____

_____.

4. *Those who are anointed comfort those who mourn (Matt. 5:4).*

The comfort we have received from the Lord, we must share with others (2 Cor. 1) because the Comforter within us comforts the comfortless of the world in the anointed place of service.

To whom is the Spirit leading you to comfort? _____

_____

> *The anointed place of service is that place where the Spirit leads us for the purpose of pouring out His healing oil.*

Ask Yourself . . .

❖ Are you a vessel of Christ's healing?

❖ Where is the Spirit leading you to minister? Who does He desire you to serve?

Write a prayer asking God's Spirit to anoint you and send you for service:

_____

_____

_____

_____

_____

*O*ne of the Pharisees asked Jesus to come to his home for a meal, so Jesus accepted the invitation and sat down to eat. A certain immoral woman heard he was there and brought a beautiful jar filled with expensive perfume. Then she knelt behind him at his feet, weeping. Her tears fell on his feet, and she wiped them off with her hair. Then she kept kissing his feet and putting perfume on them. Then he turned to the woman and said to Simon, "Look at this woman kneeling here. When I entered your home, you didn't offer me water to wash the dust from my feet, but she has washed them with her tears and wiped them with her hair. You didn't give me a kiss of greeting, but she has kissed my feet again and again from the time I first came in. You neglected the courtesy of olive oil to anoint my head, but she has anointed my feet with rare perfume" (Luke 7:36–38, 44–46).

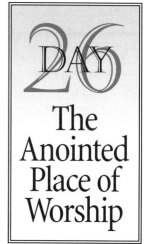

DAY 26

The Anointed Place of Worship

This repentant woman knew that the anointed place of worship begins at the feet of Jesus. She knew to bow down and worship Him. And so do we, because we understand that He gave up everything in heaven (Phil. 2) to save us here on earth. Watching this woman anoint His feet, Jesus said, "I tell you, her sins—and they are many—have been forgiven, so she has shown me much love" (Luke 7:47).

We anoint Jesus with our worship out of our deepest love knowing that we have been forgiven and are greatly loved by Him.

The anointed place of worship has nothing to do with ritual, religion, or rite. This immoral woman was in the wrong place (among hard-hearted legalists) doing the wrong thing (touching a rabbi's feet!) in the wrong way (kissing His feet and perfuming them, before wiping them with her hair). And her worship was too costly from a human perspective. But from God's perspective this woman poured herself out in humility as a holy drink offering, and Jesus extolled her for it.

Isn't it interesting how Jesus used women as examples for teaching the true nature of worship? In the Old Covenant, women had very little to do with worship, because men officiated at the altar. But in the New Covenant, Jesus shattered the gender gap by lifting women up as persons of exemplary dignity and worth. Read the following passages about women in the Gospels, then write down what they reveal about women and worship:

The praying woman (Luke 1:5–25) _____

_____.

The blessed woman (Luke 1:26–38) _____

_____

The prophetic woman (Luke 2:36–38) _____

_____

The sinful woman (Luke 7:36–50) _____

_____

The women who followed (Luke 8:1–3) _____

_____

The sick woman (Luke 8:40–48) _____

_____

The sisters—working and worshiping (Luke 10:38–42)_____

_____

The persistent widow (Luke 18:1–8) _____

_____

The giving widow (Luke 21:1–4) _____

_____

The Gentile woman (Mark 7:24–30) _____

_____

The believing sisters (John 11:1–44) _____

_____

The grieving women (Luke 24:1–7) _____

_____

The proclaiming women (Luke 24:8–12) _____

_____

The anointed place of worship is worshiping God as He desires—in Spirit and in truth.

Ask Yourself . . .

❖ What distracts you from worship?

❖ Are you more concerned with style than substance in your worship of God?

Write a prayer worshiping the Lord in the anointing of the Spirit:

_____

_____

S *o there at Hebron David made a covenant with the leaders of Israel before the Lord. They anointed him king of Israel, just as the Lord had promised through Samuel (1 Chron. 11:3).*

DAY 27

The Anointed Place of Leadership

David was God's chosen anointed leader over the nation of Israel. The former shepherd boy's anointing was recognized by the prophet Samuel, by Israel's army, and by the leaders of the nation. And it would be from the house of David several centuries later that the Anointed One—Jesus would come to lead every nation under the sun.

The anointed leader has certain qualities that were epitomized in the lives of King David and the King of kings, Jesus. Below are passages from both of their lives that reveal their leadership qualities. Look up the passages then write down the qualities.

David and the Son of David	Anointed Leaders are:
1 Samuel 13:14	_____
Psalm 51:14	_____
Psalm 110	_____
Mark 10:43	_____
Luke 9:48	_____
Matthew 20:27	
Isaiah 53:11	_____

The anointed place of leadership is wherever the Anointed One places those He has chosen to lead.

To lead in the kingdom of God is to continually seek and serve the Lord while always being careful to give all the glory to Him.

In reflecting on the life and ministry of the Anointed One, rank the following qualities from Jesus' life in the order of their importance to leadership:

_____ Love and compassion for others.

_____ Servant leadership.

_____ Willingness to listen.

_____ Wise understanding and knowledge.

_____ Ability to teach and to live the teaching.

_____ Vulnerable and transparent.

_____ Truthful and makes right choices.

_____ Disciplined spiritually.

_____ Holy and pure.

_____ Seeks first the kingdom of God.

_____ Willing to lay down His life for others.

_____ Other:_____.

The anointing on Jesus' ministry set the standard for all ministry and leadership. His anointing for leadership has been described as *descending into greatness.* Read Philippians 2:5–11 and underline the phrase that best describes the anointing you want on your leadership:

The Anointed Leader . . .

> *Your attitude should be the same that Christ Jesus had. Though he was God, he did not demand and cling to his rights as God. He made himself nothing; he took the humble position of a slave and appeared in human form. And in human form he obediently humbled himself even further by dying a criminal's death on a cross. Because of this, God raised him up to the heights of heaven and gave him a name that is above every other name, so that at the name of Jesus every knee will bow, in heaven and on earth and under the earth, and every tongue will confess that Jesus Christ is Lord, to the glory of God the Father. —Philippians 2:5–11*

Ask Yourself . . .

❖ As a leader, how are you serving others?

❖ Have you descended from your pride into servanthood?

> *Write a prayer asking Christ's anointing for leadership to be birthed in you:*

_____

_____

*H*e told them, "The man they call Jesus made mud and smoothed it over my eyes and told me, 'Go to the pool of Siloam and wash off the mud.' I went and washed, and now I can see!" (John 9:11).

Jesus anointed this blind man's eyes at the pool of Siloam, and he received sight. Christ took something in the natural—common dirt mixed with water—used it supernaturally to heal—and the blind man could see. In a parallel way we are naturally blind to the things of God's Spirit until Jesus anoints us to see.

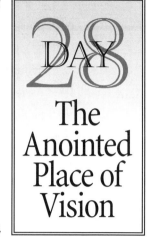

DAY 28

The Anointed Place of Vision

In the natural, the man at the pool was blind until Jesus anointed his eyes. In the same way, spiritually, we are blind to the things of the Spirit until Jesus anoints us to see. Things that look impossible in the natural become possible when we are anointed as Christ's natural places, or vessels, of vision to help others see spiritually.

God's anointed vision sees everything from His perspective. The Spirit's vision goes beyond the limits of time and space, and transcends human boundaries.

Anointed vision sees with the eyes of the Spirit.

Just as the blind man needed Jesus to anoint his eyes for natural sight, we need Christ to anoint our spiritual eyes to see spiritual sights. And because Jesus taught, "God blesses those whose hearts are pure, for they will see God" (Matt. 5:8)—we can know that the optic nerve for spiritual sight is directly connected to a pure heart.

How clearly are you seeing God and His vision for your life? Below is a pair of glasses representing vision. Shade the lens to the degree you are clearly seeing God's vision for your life. (For example, if you are barely seeing His vision then you might shade them 80 or 90 percent.)

The Spirit's anointing of vision gives us the ability to see God's vision clearly and inspires us to interact with what we see. But the clarity of God's vision in you depends on the purity of your heart. On the graph below, shade to the level of your heart's purity in each area of your life:

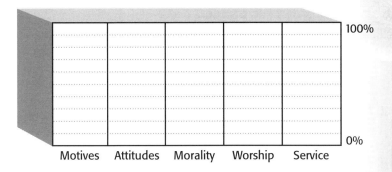

| | Motives | Attitudes | Morality | Worship | Service | 100% 0% |

To see with the Father's eyes requires Christ to anoint our eyes as His place, or location of perspective for others as well as ourselves. When people visit your house they should know it as an anointed place where they can spiritually see.

Ask Yourself . . .

❖ Are you willing to be Christ's natural vessel that He anoints supernaturally to see the truths of His Spirit to help others believe and see?

❖ How has the Spirit changed your vision of yourself and others since you have known Jesus as Savior and Lord?

Write a prayer asking Jesus to anoint your natural eyes with His spiritual vision:

_____

_____

_____

_____

_____

*T*he kings of the earth prepare for battle; the rulers plot together against the Lord and against his anointed one (Ps. 2:2).

The anointing of God's Spirit is costly. Jesus Christ, God's Anointed One, paid the high price of our anointing with His suffering and death on the cross. And when all the principalities and powers of this world attempted to destroy the anointing at Calvary, they failed! But they did attempt to do it.

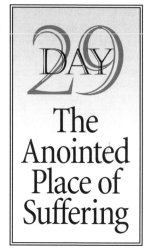

DAY 29

The Anointed Place of Suffering

Jesus taught, "God blesses those who are persecuted because they live for God, for the Kingdom of heaven is theirs. God blesses you when you are mocked and persecuted and lied about because you are my followers" (Matt. 5:10–11). So when we choose to follow the Anointed One, we will be persecuted. Sometimes our price for the anointing once we have received Him is suffering and persecution.

> *If we are to share in Christ's anointing, we must also partake in His suffering.*

Read, then write down what the following scriptures reveal about suffering and persecution.

Mark 14:36 _____

Acts 20:23 _____

Romans 8:17 _____

2 Corinthians 1:5–7 _____

2 Corinthians 4:10 _____

Philippians 1:29–30; 3:10 _____

2 Timothy 4:5 _____

1 Peter 2:20, 4:13 _____

Suffering with Christ can bring us into one of the deepest levels of His anointing available in life. How? Suffering refines our faith (1 Peter 1) and enables us to understand the sufferings of others as we comfort them (2 Cor. 1). That's why Paul wrote in 1 Corinthians 12:26, "If one part [of the body] suffers, all the parts suffer with it, and if one part is honored, all the parts are glad."

Check all the ways below you have experienced the anointed place of **suffering** as you've ministered Christ's comfort to others:

❑ Praying with those suffering.

❑ Crying with those suffering.

❑ Being with those suffering.

❑ Listening to those suffering.

❑ Caring for the physical needs of those suffering.

❑ Binding up the emotional wounds of those suffering.

❑ Encouraging and edifying those suffering.

❑ Taking the suffering of others upon yourself.

❑ Other: _____.

The anointed place of suffering is the cross. So when we take up our cross to follow Christ, we will enter into His suffering to minister in His name.

Ask Yourself . . .

❖ To whom have you been ministering lately who has struggled with emotional or physical suffering?

❖ How do you believe suffering empowers you to enter into the anointing of Christ's sufferings?

Write a prayer asking Christ for the strength and faith to suffer with Him:

_____

_____

_____

_____

_____

O God, look with favor upon the king, our protector! Have mercy upon the one you anointed (Ps. 84:9).

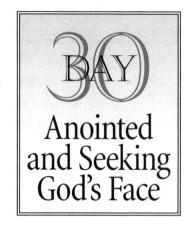

Anointed and Seeking God's Face

David's psalms of worship continually sought the face of God (Ps. 105:4). Because when a child of God stays before God's face like David, we are continually drawn to keep seeking the presence and anointing of God.

We are anointed in His presence. We encounter the richness of God's grace and mercy in His presence. So when you feel weak and far removed from His anointing, seek His face. Because God's mercy and anointing always flows when His people seek His face (2 Chron. 7:14).

But for David, being anointed was not enough. The Hebrew patriarch recognized his need to seek God's face continually to constantly experience His presence. Because apart from His presence, no anointing exists.

Take some time now to reflect back on what you've learned in this devotional study by completing the following sentences:

I encounter the Spirit's anointing whenever I _____

_____ .

His anointing on me as a royal priest empowers me to _____

_____ .

My life has been changed by the power of His anointing in that _____

_____ .

I most need the oil of _____

_____ .

In Christ, the Spirit has anointed me to _____

_____ .

When I serve others, I encounter the Spirit's anointing through the gifts of_____

_____ .

I need to seek God's face and encounter His anointing especially when I _____

_____ .

The anointing of the Holy Spirit empowers believers to worship, minister, lead, and pray. Apart from His anointing, we are powerless to serve and minister. But as ministers of His anointing, signs and wonders manifest to give witness to the glory of God's Anointed One, the Messiah, Jesus Christ.

Write a prayer praising Jesus for the anointing He has poured out upon your life:

_____

_____

_____

_____

_____

You can continue your encounters with the Holy Spirit by using the other devotional study guides listed at the end of this booklet, and by using the companion *Holy Spirit Encounter Bible.*

Leader's Guide

For Group Sessions

This devotional study is an excellent resource for group study including such settings as:

❖ Sunday school classes and other church classes
❖ Prayer groups
❖ Bible study groups
❖ Ministries involving small groups, home groups, and accountability groups
❖ Study groups for youth and adults

Before the First Session

❖ Contact everyone interested in participating in your group to inform them about the meeting time, date, and place.
❖ Make certain that everyone has a copy of this devotional study guide.
❖ Plan out all your teaching lessons before starting the first session. Also ask group members to begin their daily encounters in this guide. While each session will not strictly adhere to a seven-day schedule, group members who faithful study a devotional every day will be prepared to share in the group sessions.
❖ Pray for the Holy Spirit to guide, teach, and help each participant.
❖ Be certain the place where you meet has a chalkboard, white board, or flipchart with appropriate writing materials.

Planning the Group Sessions

1. You will have four sessions together as a group. So plan to cover at least seven days in each session. If your sessions are weekly, ask the participants to complete the final two days before the last session.

2. In your first session, have group members find a partner with whom they will share and pray each time you meet. Keep the same pairs throughout the group sessions. See if you can randomly put pairs together—men with men, and women with women.

3. Have group and class members complete their devotional studies prior to their group sessions to enhance group sharing, study, and prayer. Begin each session with prayer.

4. Either the group leader or selected members should read the key Scriptures from each of the seven daily devotionals you will be studying in the session.

5. As the leader, you should decide which exercises and questions are to be covered prior to each session.

6. Also decide which exercises and sessions will be most appropriate to share with the group as a whole, or in pairs.

7. Decide which prayer(s) from the seven devotionals you will want the pairs to pray with one another.

8. Close each session by giving every group member the opportunity to share with the group how he or she encountered the Holy Spirit during the previous week. Then lead the group in prayer or have group members pray aloud in a prayer circle as you close the session.

9. You will have nine days of devotionals to study in the last session. So, use the last day as an in-depth sharing time in pairs. Invite all the group members to share the most important thing they learned about the Holy Spirit's anointing during this study and how their relationship with the Spirit was deepened because of it. Close with prayers of praise and thanksgiving.

10. Remember to allow each person the freedom "not to share" with their prayer partner or in public if they are uncomfortable with it.

11. Always start and end each group session on time and seek to keep them no longer than ninety minutes.

12. Finally, be careful. This is not a therapy group. Group members who seek to dominate group discussions with their own problems or questions should be ministered to by the group leader or pastor one-on-one outside of the group session.

Titles in the Holy Spirit Encounter Guide Series

Additional Notes

Additional Notes

Additional Notes

Additional Notes

Additional Notes

Additional Notes

Additional Notes

Additional Notes

Additional Notes

Additional Notes